MIRROR WITH A MEMORY

Mirror
with a Memory

• A Nation's Story in Photographs •

• JANICE WEAVER •

TUNDRA BOOKS

Text copyright © 2007 by Janice Weaver

Published in Canada by Tundra Books,
75 Sherbourne Street, Toronto, Ontario
M5A 2P9

Published in the United States by
Tundra Books of Northern New York,
P.O. Box 1030, Plattsburgh,
New York 12901

Library of Congress Control Number:
2006906055

The title of this book is drawn from "The
Stereoscope and the Stereograph" by Oliver
Wendell Holmes, Sr., published in the June
1859 issue of *The Atlantic Monthly*.

Library and Archives Canada Cataloguing in Publication

Weaver, Janice
    Mirror with a memory : a nation's story in photographs /
    Janice Weaver.

Includes index.
ISBN-13: 978-0-88776-747-0
ISBN-10: 0-88776-747-8

    I. Canada – Pictorial works. I. Title.

FC59.W415 2007 971'.00222   C2006-903680-2

We acknowledge the financial support of the Government of Canada
through the Book Publishing Industry Development Program (BPIDP)
and that of the Government of Ontario through the Ontario Media
Development Corporation's Ontario Book Initiative. We further
acknowledge the support of the Canada Council for the Arts and
the Ontario Arts Council for our publishing program.

ONTARIO ARTS COUNCIL
CONSEIL DES ARTS DE L'ONTARIO

Design: Jennifer Lum / Kong Njo

Printed and bound in China

1 2 3 4 5 6   12 11 10 09 08 07

Contents

INTRODUCTION

When cameras were first invented, people didn't know quite what to make of them. In their ability to capture an exact moment of time – to take a specific instant and hold it forever – they were unlike anything that had ever come before. Painters could recreate events after the fact, but photographers could capture the precise second when those events actually took place. One writer, describing this extraordinary new invention in an American magazine, called the camera "a mirror with a memory." It was, he said, "the most audacious [and] incredible . . . of all the discoveries man has made."

Like a mirror, the camera reflects the world around us, showing us people and things as they really are. Every photograph depicts something that exists or did exist – something that actually happened. But behind every photograph there stands a photographer, someone who is making decisions about what to put in and what to leave out, what to draw attention to and what to ignore. And because of that, the camera – again like a mirror – can distort the truth.

It's important to see photographs for what they are. They have an astonishing ability, in the words of Edward Steichen, a famous American photographer, to record "feelings written on the human face, the beauty of the earth and skies that man has inherited, and the wealth and confusion man has created." They allow us to look into the lives of people who lived decades, or even a century, before us, and that lets us experience events that we haven't lived through ourselves. We can look at a photograph and imagine what it's like to be on a prairie farm with a dust storm bearing down on us, or to be struggling up the steep incline of the Chilkoot Pass. A picture truly is worth a thousand words, and photographs can bring events to life in a way that words often cannot.

At the same time, photographs are sometimes used as propaganda to promote a certain belief or position or to express an untruth. First World War photographers depicted Canadian soldiers bravely charging into battle so that people back home wouldn't lose faith in the war effort. An early photograph of the elaborate Parliament Buildings under construction advanced the idea that Canada was a sophisticated, highly developed nation. Photographs of some neat and orderly North-West Mounted Police barracks in Alberta reinforced the impression that the Mounties were in control of the Canadian West.

Because Canada is such a young country, its whole story as a nation can be told through photographs. The country came into existence at around the same time as photography did – in the middle of the 1800s – and the two grew and evolved together. The earliest Canadian photographs were stiff, posed portraits of well-off members of the middle class – successful people who were probably

Say Cheese!

The first practical photographs were known as daguerreotypes, after their inventor, the Frenchman Louis Daguerre. Daguerreotypes reduced the exposure time for photographs from several hours to about ten to fifteen minutes (and eventually to less than a minute). To get a good, crisp photograph, those posing – sometimes called "patients" – had to sit perfectly still while the negative was being exposed to light. The slightest bit of movement would show up as blurred streaks in the finished piece. But just imagine trying to sit completely still for ten or fifteen minutes. No wonder people in old photographs are seldom smiling!

Early photographers quickly developed some crucial tricks of the trade to ensure that their customers would be happy with the finished product. They would keep cotton batting on hand to fill out sunken cheeks, wax to paste back prominent ears, and even vises to hold heads steady. Not surprisingly, many of them developed a preference for photographing the dead, who held still so much better than live subjects did!

The Shutterbugs

Probably the most famous Canadian photographer was William Notman, a Scottish immigrant who opened his first studio in Montreal in 1856. Notman became famous for his portraits and his depictions of daily life in Canada. He took high-quality photographs of ordinary people at work — soldiers and sailors, lumberjacks, newsboys and shopkeepers — as well as formal studio portraits of the well-to-do.

At his shops in Ottawa, Toronto, and Halifax, Notman employed several men who became well-known photographers in their own right, including Alexander Henderson, who specialized in romantic shots of the landscape, such as the famous photo of the Montmorency ice cone in the "Fun and Games" chapter; William James Topley, who created portraits of Canadian political leaders in the Ottawa studio; and Notman's son, William McFarlane Notman, who is best known for his pictures of the Canadian Pacific Railway and the vistas of the Canadian West, including the photograph that opens this introduction.

not quite wealthy enough to hire an artist to paint them. But soon, photography had advanced sufficiently that it could move out of the studio and into the streets to record important events – from D'Arcy McGee's funeral to the Northwest Rebellion – as they happened.

Less bulky equipment and shorter exposure times also made it possible for photographers to put their skills to use documenting the growth of this country. They travelled with the Geological Survey of Canada, the North American Boundary Commission, and the Dominion Lands Survey to record the country's borders, map its geography, and search out the best areas for future settlement and expansion. Photographers went along on Arctic expeditions, helping to establish Canada's rights to the Far North, and they were there as the Canadian Pacific Railway was built, helping to promote the country as a tourist destination. Immigration agents even used photographs of Canada's wild and beautiful landscape and its many thriving farms to entice Europeans to move here for a better life.

Photography has played a significant role in the development of this country, and in helping us define and understand ourselves. It's a superb medium of communication – a vehicle for sharing triumphs and tragedies, for celebrating achievements, and for commemorating disasters – and it has given us a deeper understanding of the story we share as Canadians. It has changed how we look at the world and has touched all our lives in the simplest and most profound ways.

Building a Nation

Canada in the Beginning

In the 1700s, the powerful British Empire controlled virtually all of settled North America. Its colonies stretched from the American South to Newfoundland to Hudson Bay. But in 1775, a revolution erupted in the thirteen American colonies, and Britain lost its hold on them. All that was left was the northern half of North America, a hodgepodge of territories that seemed condemned by its own geography. In the centre sat what would become Quebec and Ontario — the two quickly growing halves of the United Province of Canada. Far out in the west, cut off by the towering Rocky Mountains, was British Columbia. In the east, divided by perilous ocean waters, were the Maritimes. And then there was the endless expanse of the prairies — not to mention the frigid, mysterious North.

The idea of uniting all of Britain's remaining colonies into one nation called Canada took hold at the Confederation

Conference in 1864. It was a bold, almost unimaginable notion, and if they'd really understood what it would take to shape these territories into one country, the Fathers of Confederation — the men who took on the task — might have thought twice about trying it. A long, tough road lay ahead. There would be hard-fought battles over where to establish the new nation's capital, where to place the border with the United States, and where to put the railway that would eventually tie the country together. There would be bitter clashes with Natives and Métis (people of mixed French and Indian ancestry), and with American traders tempted by the promised riches of Canada's abundant natural resources. And there would be daring exploits and adventures — fortune hunters scaling snow-covered Yukon peaks, mariners setting sail for uncharted Arctic waters, and immigrants packing up all their worldly goods and heading for a new life on the far side of the globe.

All in all, Confederation was a wild and brave experiment in creating a nation from many distinct territories and peoples. One opponent compared it to trying to unite Scotland with Poland and Hungary — a mad idea that was doomed to fail. But the true believers fought on, and on July 1, 1867, they had their new nation. "The days of isolation . . . are past," cried one Halifax newspaper. "Henceforth we are a united people, and the greatness of each goes to swell the greatness of the whole."

What better place to begin than in Charlottetown, Prince Edward Island, at the Confederation Conference of 1864? These twenty-five men — often called the Fathers of Confederation — are delegates from PEI, Nova Scotia, New Brunswick, and the United Province of Canada (Quebec and Ontario). Grouped stiffly on the steps of the lieutenant-governor's residence, they have come together to record the historic moment when Canada was born. One man just to the right of the door doffs his tall stovepipe hat, perhaps saluting the new nation they've created.

Back in 1859, construction had begun on the Parliament Buildings for the United Province of Canada. Many people thought Ottawa was a terrible choice for a capital city, though. In those days, it was still an unruly frontier town full of lumbermen and restless soldiers guarding the Ottawa River against American invaders intent on seizing this country for themselves. People in the much larger and — at least in their eyes — more sophisticated cities of Toronto and Montreal thought Ottawa was little more than a mosquito-infested backwater. But Queen Victoria, who was asked to choose the capital, selected the town over both Toronto and Montreal, and over Kingston and Quebec City as well. Some claimed that she'd made her choice by closing her eyes and picking a random spot on a map, and had no real idea what she'd done. But in fact, Ottawa was a very wise pick. It had a mixed population of English and French, and it sat right on the border of the former Upper Canada (Ontario) and Lower Canada (Quebec). Best of all, it was already connected by rail to Toronto, Montreal, Boston, and New York, and it was easily accessible by water as well.

Eight years later, at the time of Confederation, the argument about the capital erupted all over again. But the Parliament Buildings had already been built, and there seemed to be no good reason to start again somewhere else. By then, most people simply wanted to get on with the job of building a great and prosperous nation.

Where did the United States end and Canada begin? In the late 1850s, engineers from the North American Boundary Commission set out to mark the exact border, all the way from the Pacific Ocean to the other side of the Rocky Mountains. But while it's easy to draw a line on a map, it's very hard work to carve a border out of dense forest, as these tired, scruffy-looking men are doing. It took the engineers four gruelling years just to make their way across British Columbia and over the mountains to the foothills of Alberta.

In the early 1860s the American Civil War interrupted the work of the boundary commission, but by the 1870s the engineers were able to set out once more, pushing their way east to the Lake of the Woods, on the border between Manitoba and Ontario. On the prairies, where trees were few and far between, the men built prehistoric-looking earthen boundary mounds to mark the border. Although the surveyors found the prairie landscape easier to cross, they faced new challenges, including drought conditions and, at one point, a swarm of grasshoppers that rained from the sky like an April downpour.

The engineers of the boundary commission took some remarkable photographs, including this one showing the bones of several dead Crow Indians. For many people, this photo – with an armed white man sitting casually among the skeletons – was a symbol of the sometimes violent way that white settlers took control of the West. In fact, though, these Crow warriors had been killed by a group of rival Blackfoot, and the picture was no evidence at all of clashes between Natives and whites. As grim as it is, it's just one more record of the boundary commission's push across the prairies.

It wasn't unusual to see thousands of sun-bleached buffalo bones littering the prairie ground like the aftermath of some gruesome snowstorm. The buffalo hunt was a traditional way of life for Plains Natives and Métis. But when horses and rifles came to the prairies, and hunters learned to use corrals and buffalo jumps to slaughter the animals in huge numbers, the great herds began to decline. By the 1880s, when this photo was taken, there were only about a thousand buffalo left – of the sixty million that had once roamed the land.

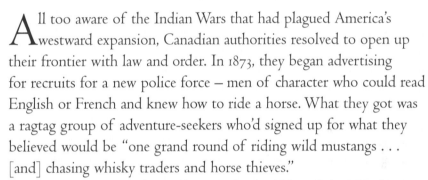

All too aware of the Indian Wars that had plagued America's westward expansion, Canadian authorities resolved to open up their frontier with law and order. In 1873, they began advertising for recruits for a new police force — men of character who could read English or French and knew how to ride a horse. What they got was a ragtag group of adventure-seekers who'd signed up for what they believed would be "one grand round of riding wild mustangs . . . [and] chasing whisky traders and horse thieves."

In July 1874, the first officers and constables of the North-West Mounted Police (renamed the Royal Canadian Mounted Police, or RCMP, in 1920) set out from Dufferin, Manitoba, on an epic march across the prairies. With oxen, cattle, and two-wheeled carts in tow, they inched their way forward, arriving at Fort Macleod, near present-day Calgary, almost three months later. Once there, they began to patrol the border, suppressing the whisky trade and establishing Canada's control over the region.

"Though [the Mounties] were only of a number you could count on your fingers and toes," remembered one Native chief, "the cutthroats and criminals who recognized no authority but their guns, who killed each other on the slightest pretence and murdered Indians without fear of reprisal, immediately abandoned their forts . . . and fled back to their own side of the line. . . . It was the power that stands behind those few Red Coats that those men feared."

The promise of a rail link to the East had enticed the isolated colony of British Columbia – which shared closer ties with the United States – to join Canada in 1871. But actually building that link proved to be a greater challenge than anyone had imagined. Even the job of charting the route for the Canadian Pacific Railway (CPR) was enormous. Surveyors had to scramble up rocky outcroppings – as these two men from the Dominion Lands Survey office are doing – scale mountains that had never been climbed, and find their way through enormous stretches of unmapped land, carrying all their equipment and supplies with them.

WHITE CREEK BRIDGE AND 4 TUNNELS, NEAR SPUZZUM, B.C.

Then came the enormous job of building the rail line. When they couldn't go over or around the Rocky Mountains, the railway crews had to find a way to go through them. For the most part, this dangerous work was left to thousands of Chinese labourers who'd been brought in to ensure that the CPR line got finished. These men used liquid nitroglycerine to blast their way through the stubborn rock. For about a dollar a day, they pressed forward through the Fraser Canyon, risking rock slides, tunnel collapses, and premature explosions. In this photograph, one tunnel near the town of Spuzzum frames the view, while the mouths to three more can be seen stretching off into the distance.

Crews laid railway track from both directions, east and west, and finally met at Craigellachie, British Columbia, in November 1885. In what is perhaps the most famous photograph in Canadian history, Donald A. Smith, a major financial backer of the CPR, gets ready to hammer home the last spike and bring the project to its close. In an odd bit of irony for the problem-plagued railway – which was dogged by accidents and deaths and constantly teetered on the brink of bankruptcy – Smith's first blow bent the spike so badly that it had to be taken out and replaced.

After all the wealthy investors and dignitaries had gone, dozens of ordinary workers convinced the photographer to stay behind for one final shot — their own version of the famous "last spike." (Still absent are the Chinese labourers who laid the most treacherous sections of track.) The construction of the CPR was such a dangerous venture that some denounced it as "an act of insane recklessness," but it remains one of the major engineering feats of all time. These men knew they had been part of something great, and in fact, the railway proved to be exactly what its champions had said it would be: a ribbon of steel knitting together our vast nation.

In 1896, gold was discovered in the Klondike region of the Yukon. When news reached the outside world in 1897, people raced north by the tens of thousands, eager to make their fortunes. Many gold seekers spent months — even years — finding their way there, with most struggling over the legendary Chilkoot Pass. (Those who could afford it sailed up the coast and into Dawson in the luxury of a steamship instead.) The prospectors didn't know that most of the richest claims had been staked long before word of the strike got out. Entrepreneurs like Mr. Lubelski, the owner of what passed for a first-class hotel in Dawson, had by far the better idea. Merchants and saloon keepers and wilderness guides were among the few who actually made money from the gold rush.

These fortune seekers are just a few hundred of the estimated twenty to thirty thousand who struggled up the 1,000-metre (3,500-foot) Chilkoot Pass and down the Yukon River to Dawson. Canadian authorities, anxious to impose order and assert Canada's sovereignty in the region, set up a customs station and a North-West Mounted Police post at the summit of the pass. Every would-be miner who wanted to be allowed into the Klondike had to carry with him a full year's worth of supplies. For most prospectors, this meant making as many as fifty exhausting trips up and down the Chilkoot Trail.

Having built the railway and established the rule of law in the West, Canadians turned their attention to their harshest, most challenging frontier, the Far North. In 1880, the British had ceded the Arctic islands to Canada, but the government was slow to assert its authority. When rumours began to fly that American polar explorers intended to claim the islands for their own country, the Canadian government finally took action.

This photograph shows the majestic-looking *Arctic*, captained by Joseph-Elzéar Bernier, preparing to set sail from Quebec City for the Far North in 1908. As an agent for the government, Bernier issued permits to whalers and fishermen, and collected duties from them. He also helped establish several North-West Mounted Police posts in the region and completed numerous surveys of the land. His expeditions ensured that Canada had a regular presence in the North — something that's required by international law before a nation can claim sovereignty over an area. In 1909, Bernier made the claim more clearly, unveiling on remote Melville Island a plaque declaring that all the Arctic islands belonged to Canada.

Over the years, Bernier made a dozen trips to the Far North, and they allowed Canada to lay claim to about 740,000 square kilometres (285,000 square miles) of territory. He has been called the greatest Canadian navigator of all time.

With Canada now officially stretching from sea to sea to sea, the government began advertising for newcomers to fill the expanse of land within those borders. People from all parts of Europe were encouraged to come. If they knew how to farm and thought they could endure the challenges of a prairie winter, so much the better. These recent arrivals – possibly members of one extended family – posed for a quick photo at Toronto's Union Station before they departed for places unknown. Their faces tell a story of mixed emotions – hope, excitement, caution, and fear. But they all look determined to build a new life that will justify their long and dangerous journey here.

Among the newcomers were about a hundred thousand children –
some as young as four or five years old – who'd been shipped from
the most poverty-plagued areas of London, England, for supposedly
unlimited opportunities in Canada. Once here, many of these "home
children" found themselves in a kind of indentured servitude – doing
hard physical labour on remote farms for little or no money. Of all
these wary, expectant children, which ones found the happy lives they
had been promised?

Storm and Strife

Canada in Times of Trouble

I t is often said that Canada was founded on the principles of peace, order, and good government. Compared to the United States – which achieved its independence only after a violent revolution, engaged in a series of brutal clashes with its Native population, and suffered a civil war that tore the country apart – Canada has had a remarkably trouble-free ride through history. We came to nationhood not through confrontation and bloodshed, but by persuading provinces to sign on with promises of new railways and debt relief. We gained our independence from Britain not through revolution, but by debating and negotiating terms. Whenever conflict arose, Canadians were more likely to turn to the courts than to the battlefields.

It hasn't all been smooth sailing, however. Manitoba's entry into Confederation was marked by the sometimes violent resistance of Native and Métis groups. The fight to make Quebec independent has, at times, flared into bomb blasts and kidnappings. We've grappled with catastrophes like a deadly influenza epidemic and mass unemployment, and we've seen whole cities shut down by striking workers. Racism has cast — and continues to cast — a shadow over our lives, and too many of our Natives still struggle to be treated with respect and to create a meaningful, hopeful future for their children.

Canada is an immense country. We couldn't dream of uniting that much geography, and three distinct (and often feuding) founding nations — the English, the French, and the aboriginal peoples — without some discord. Even so, the Canadian way seems to be to solve conflict with compromise, to seek common ground rather than to retreat into difference. Prime Minister Wilfrid Laurier — a French Canadian who was a great promoter of Confederation and national unity — knew from first-hand experience how difficult it sometimes was to locate that common ground. "I am branded in Quebec as a traitor to the French, and in Ontario as a traitor to the English," he once complained. "I am neither. I am a Canadian. . . . I have had before me as a pillar of fire by night and a pillar of cloud by day a policy of true Canadianism, of moderation, of conciliation."

Having emigrated from Ireland, which was struggling under British rule, Thomas D'Arcy McGee was determined to build Canada into a nation where all people could live in harmony. "I see in the not remote distance," he declared, "one great nationality bound by the blue rim of the ocean." A writer and politician of tremendous eloquence and passion, McGee became one of the leading promoters of Confederation. Sadly, he was shot dead in 1868, in one of the few political assassinations this country has suffered. Here, his elaborate, Victorian-style funeral procession crawls through the streets of Montreal, while on the far left a macabre sign advertises coffins for sale.

Canada had made a deal with Louis Riel, the ambitious and charismatic leader of the Métis people, to end an uprising and bring Manitoba into Confederation in 1870. But the government's promises of land and protections for the French-speaking Métis were never honoured, and in 1885 a second rebellion broke out, at the town of Batoche, Saskatchewan. This time, Riel, who'd been forced into exile in the United States after the first revolt, was determined to give his people a great victory.

The Métis were skilled fighters who used their knowledge of the land to their advantage – digging rifle pits and trenches, and lying in wait for their foe. "This was a rather different way of fighting from what we had expected," wrote one soldier of his first contact with the rebels. "We calculated on seeing the enemy anyway. We were all fully under the impression that in aiming our rifles we would have something to aim at." With smart fighting, the Métis enjoyed encouraging early victories at Duck Lake and Fish Creek.

But the world had changed since Riel's limited triumph in 1870 – not least because of the new railway, which made it possible for the government to ship troops to the prairies from Toronto and Ottawa in a fraction of the time it once took. Within eleven days of the first shots fired, soldiers had unloaded at the Qu'Appelle station and started slowly marching across the valley towards Batoche, reclaiming territory as they went. By the time the troops reached the town itself, the Northwest Rebellion was all but over. Gravely outnumbered, the Métis were soon surrounded and Riel was quickly captured, bringing his second uprising to an end.

These soldiers may look as if they don't have a care in the world, but in fact they're in the middle of a critical assignment: they're transporting Louis Riel halfway across Saskatchewan, from Swift Current to Regina, to stand trial for treason. This photo – like the ones on the previous and facing pages – was taken by an American named O. B. Buell, a self-proclaimed professor of photography who created an extraordinary visual record of Riel's rebellion and the construction of the Canadian Pacific Railway. Buell's photographs gave ordinary Canadians a remarkable glimpse into the sometimes dangerous work of opening up the West.

Riel spoke in his own defence during his trial in a sweltering Regina courtroom in 1885. His long, rambling speech was disturbing to many, but it had moments of near poetry as well. "I know that through the grace of God," he declared, "I am the founder of Manitoba. . . . I believe by what I suffered for fifteen years, by what I have done for Manitoba and the people of the North-West, that my words are worth something." The jury found him guilty of treason but thought he was a little mad, so they asked the judge not to sentence him to death. Riel was hanged just the same. More than a century would pass before Parliament overturned his conviction, and finally recognized him as one of Canada's founding fathers.

When Canadian soldiers came home from the First World War, they brought more than victory with them. They also carried the "Spanish flu," a highly infectious disease that attacked as many young, healthy people as it did very old and very weak ones. A desperate nation tried everything to halt the spread of the disease. Many schools and other public places where people gathered in large numbers were shut down. Some communities passed laws that made it a criminal offence to shake hands. And everywhere people went, they wore masks, as these employees of a Calgary bank are doing.

But these efforts could only slow the flu's relentless march. It killed fifty thousand Canadians — almost as many as had died in the dank, filthy trenches of the war's front lines, where the flu had apparently been born. In the hardest-hit areas of Quebec and Labrador, entire villages were simply wiped out. The toll worldwide was even more staggering, with the disease claiming somewhere between twenty and fifty million lives.

On the morning of May 15, 1919, the normally bustling post-war city of Winnipeg fell silent. Fifty thousand Winnipeggers — from firefighters to letter carriers — had walked off their jobs as part of the Winnipeg General Strike. They were demanding pay increases and better working conditions — things they'd gone without during the war years. When the city threatened to fire all the striking employees, and then brought in volunteers to do their jobs, the strikers lashed out. Here, they're in the midst of overturning a streetcar — an act that sparked a violent clash with the RCMP later that day.

"If we can control industrial production now, at this time," declared one strike leader, "we can control it for all time to come, and we can control the Government of this country, too." That was exactly what the government feared, and it was determined to crush the strike by any means necessary. On June 21, 1919 – a day known as "Bloody Saturday" – Mounties on horseback charged down Main Street into a swarm of striking workers, swinging at them with nightsticks. Under orders from the government, they then opened fire into the crowd, injuring thirty people and killing two.

The Great Depression, which began with the 1929 stock market
crash, was a massive economic crisis that affected the entire
world. In Canada it devastated communities from coast to coast,
but people in the West were especially hard hit. Dust storms, crop
failures, and unemployment levels that climbed above 65 percent
made it almost impossible for ordinary Canadians to survive. There
was no such thing as unemployment insurance and very little welfare,
so people without jobs had to depend on the kindness of family,
friends, even strangers. Parents like these – with seven young ones
to care for – struggled just to put food on the table and shoes on
their children's feet.

Imagine what it would be like to look up and see a dust storm like this on the horizon. Dust storms were a common sight throughout the Depression years, when drought loosened the prairie topsoil and hot summer winds whipped it up into grimy clouds known as black blizzards. The dust got everywhere, filling every nook and cranny. "A cloaking silence enveloped the whole outdoors," said one farmer's wife, describing the scene after a storm had passed, "yet dust hung in the air so thick it was clearly visible. Everything – land, air, sky – was a dull-grey colour. . . . Our feet sank in sand almost to our ankles, and we breathed and tasted the sand . . . as we walked."

One of Prime Minister R. B. Bennett's solutions to the Depression was to establish relief camps, mostly in British Columbia, for impoverished single men. The men worked for the Department of National Defence, clearing land and building roads, in exchange for meals, shelter, and a paltry twenty cents a day. The poor pay and appalling living conditions – the relief communities were called "slave camps" by those who lived there – created a lot of desperately unhappy workers, and in June 1935, hundreds of them decided to "ride the rails" to Ottawa to confront the prime minister. "We were going," explained one protester, "to lay our problems at the feet of R. B. Bennett."

The On-to-Ottawa trek quickly gained steam: men joined in at every stop along the rail line, and there were about three thousand taking part by the time the protest reached Saskatchewan. But Prime Minister Bennett had no intention of letting the men make it all the way to the nation's capital. On July 1, the RCMP was told to move in to break up a protest meeting in Regina's Market Square. Armed with baseball bats and billy clubs, the Mounties waded into the crowd, and things quickly spiralled out of control. "In less than four minutes," remembered one trekker, "Market Square was a mass of writhing, groaning forms, like a battlefield." The riot raged for hours, and when it was all over, two were dead, forty-five were injured, and more than a hundred were under arrest.

Increased immigration and conflicts over language, race, and reli[g] opened the door for the Ku Klux Klan to move into Canada from the United States in the 1920s. With few blacks to harass, Canadian Klansmen focused their wrath on Catholics, Jews, and recent arrivals from southern Europe. The Klan was never as popular here as it was south of the border, but it did attract thousands of members in Ontario, Alberta, and Saskatchewan, and rallies like the one shown here were often well attended. When Klansmen tried to blow up a Catholic church in Barrie, Ontario, however, they took things one step too far. "We do not want dynamiters in Canada," declared the judge in the case. "It is a rare and un-British crime."

White-Native relationships have traditionally been a more common source of racial tension in Canada. In this famous photograph from 1990, a young soldier and a masked Mohawk protester face off at the Kanesatake reserve near Oka, Quebec. The Mohawks had blocked a major road into Montreal to oppose a developer's plans to build a golf course on a Native burial ground. The clash exposed the mood of many Native Canadians, who'd grown tired of broken promises from Ottawa and resented their people's poor quality of life. Just two years before the standoff, one prominent Native had warned, "We may be the last generation of leaders . . . prepared to sit down and peacefully negotiate our concerns with you."

FROM HERE TO THERE

Canada on the Move

I t's impossible to exaggerate the importance of transportation to the history of Canada. In a country as vast as this, simply getting from here to there can be an immense challenge. The earliest settlers went only where their canoes would take them, navigating the lakes and rivers of eastern and central Canada. Later pioneers made their way west in covered wagons pulled by mules or oxen. And the Arctic explorers went north in great ships and sometimes had to lug their supplies across ice-choked waters on primitive sledges. All in all, Canadians have pushed into new and uncharted territory in or on just about anything that would move.

But it was the railway, more than anything else, that opened Canada to settlement and brought prosperity. It was the promise of railways that drew both British Columbia and Prince Edward Island into Confederation. And countless small cities and towns had their futures assured by rail lines that serviced their communities, while towns that were bypassed too often just dwindled and died.

The Canadian Pacific Railway, designed to link the country from coast to coast, was the boldest, most dangerous railway project in the world. It had to cross Northern Ontario's bug-infested swamps and the dense rock of the Canadian Shield, and then the vast expanses of the prairies, before it even faced the challenge of traversing the Rockies. Photographers were there to document it all, from tunnels blasted right through the mountains to hand-built wooden bridges that were among the longest and highest in the world. The pictures they took helped establish the idea of Canada as a wild and beautiful place, and encouraged new waves of immigration.

Of course, not every journey was on such an enormous scale. Quite often, Canadians struggled just to get themselves short distances in a country that sometimes seems made to impede travel instead of assist it. As late as the 1920s, it was still easy to find people who had never ventured more than a day's walk from the town where they were born – even though their ancestors had crossed half the world to get there in the first place.

With ladders and camera equipment squeezed into every available inch of space, Bill and Joe James — the sons of William James, one of Toronto's most important early photographers — dash off in search of a hot story. They're riding a slick-looking Monarch motorcycle with a wicker sidecar — probably a technological marvel for 1912, when this photo was taken. Back then, cameras were not sophisticated enough to capture movement the way they can today, so the brothers must be sitting completely still and just pretending to be on the move. Notice that the spokes on their wheels aren't even turning!

For most of the 1800s, until they were displaced by steamboats
and then the railway, Red River carts trundled slowly across the
prairies, carrying settlers to their new homes. Invented by the Métis,
these carts were built entirely of wood, which made them easy to
maintain and repair. Their two large, thick wheels were ideal for
rutted and marshy prairie fields, and the wheels could be removed
so the carts could be floated across streams or down small rivers.
But their most distinctive feature was the ear-piercing squeal they
produced as their ungreased axles creaked round and round. People
claimed they could tell whose cart was coming just by the sound of
the shriek it let loose.

They would probably have looked right at home being rowed
by Vikings through the fjords of Norway, but York boats were
uniquely Canadian. These long, flat craft originally plied the lakes
and rivers of the fur-trading areas, travelling between Hudson's Bay
Company posts, overloaded with pelts of beaver, moose, and bear.
Later, they took settlers inland in the first push into the West.
Made by Scottish boatbuilders who had been brought from the
remote Orkney Islands specifically for their skills, York boats could
be either rowed or sailed. The rough-looking sails must have meant
relief for the oarsmen — who often rowed as much as sixteen hours
a day — and they could do double duty as tents at night.

More than thirty years before the more famous Klondike Gold
Rush, rich deposits of gold were found in the remote Cariboo
Mountains, in eastern British Columbia. In 1862, in one of the stranger
transportation experiments in Canadian history, a merchant imported
about two dozen camels into the region to pack supplies up into the
goldfields. He was convinced that the camels would go days without
water or rest, carting heavy loads of supplies, just as they did in the
deserts of Asia.

But the craggy mountain trails of British Columbia were not
kind to hoofs used to soft desert sands, and the camels turned out
to be quite surly as well. They spat at and bit everyone who came near,
and ate everything they could latch their huge lips onto, from "a pair
of pants to a bar of soap," according to the Victoria *Times-Colonist*.
Worst of all, they gave off an odour so foul that it sent men running
for cover and caused horses and mules to panic and bolt. The great
experiment ended after only about four months, although some of
the camels reportedly lived on, on private farms and ranches and
even in the wild, for another forty years or so.

The first Canadian Pacific Railway transcontinental passenger train makes a brief stop on the last leg of its long journey. The train left Montreal on June 28, 1886, and arrived in Port Moody, British Columbia, the day after this photo was taken, on July 4. Not too long before, such a trip would have been almost impossible to complete. Now it could be done in just six days by anyone with a ticket and the will to travel. Wooden trestle bridges like the one seen here were a critical part of the rail line. Without them, there would have been no way for the trains to traverse the deep canyons of the Rocky Mountains. But most lasted only ten or fifteen years before they had to be replaced by sturdier versions made of steel.

Building the rail line was only the first challenge. In its early days, the CPR had to contend with money problems, high ticket prices, and too few smaller lines branching off the main route. Mother Nature didn't help matters. Avalanches and rockslides routinely rained from above, downpours washed away gravel roadbeds, and ice storms froze the tracks and even crippled the trains. This frost-covered locomotive, in a roundhouse at Rogers Pass, looks as though it's been plucked from the top of a fancy cake. After such a deep freeze, would it ever thaw out and be ready to roll again?

The railway did all the things the history books talk about — uniting the nation and opening the West to settlement — but for most people, it was just a way to see this country as they never could before. When the first prime minister, John A. Macdonald, passed through the Rockies aboard one of the very earliest transcontinental trains, his wife, Agnes, scrambled up front — *right* up front, onto the metal grille used to sweep obstacles from the tracks — for a better view. Thanks to her, riding the "cowcatcher," as this well-dressed couple are doing, became a fad that soon swept the nation.

This serious fellow looks as though he's decided not to wait for the train to make its regularly scheduled stop. In fact, he's most likely a track inspector looking for damage and signs of wear. He's riding a type of bicycle known as a velocipede, which could be powered by hand or foot pedals and was light enough to be lifted right off the tracks whenever a train appeared. A track inspector had an assigned section to patrol. He'd be out night and day — especially during and immediately after storms — looking for any little bit of disrepair that could derail a train and cause a major accident.

Many early settlers headed west with only as much baggage as they could carry or squeeze into the back of a cart. The railway, however, made it easier to move not just people but anything from a treasured locket to a grandfather clock from one end of the country to the other. Here, one family puts this brand-new technology to creative use. They're hauling their entire *house* across Manitoba for a fresh start — and perhaps some free land — in Saskatchewan or Alberta.

After Newfoundland joined Confederation in 1949, Premier Joey Smallwood began encouraging residents in the province's outports — small coastal fishing villages — to move inland. It was just too expensive to bring services like electricity and phone lines, as well as schools and hospitals, to isolated communities where only a handful of people lived. For some people, the outport closings signalled the end of a whole way of life. But others, like the ones shown here, simply set sail with their homes in tow, ready to begin again someplace new. "Everything will be okay," said one uprooted fisherman who was looking forward to modern city life. "I'm quite content. . . . Quite content of it. Me old days is over."

This 1901 picnic is unusual because the family made their trip by automobile. Cars weren't invented until the 1890s, and they didn't begin to be produced in Canada until a few years after this picture was taken. This family probably imported theirs from the United States, and getting it from Detroit to Holland, Manitoba, must have been quite an expense. This Oldsmobile was the first model in the world to be mass-produced. Back then, some people were so afraid of cars — which barrelled along at a heart-stopping three or four kilometres (about two miles) an hour — that they called them "devil wagons."

During the Depression, people often couldn't afford gas for their cars. But they still needed to get around, especially if they lived in small prairie communities with no public transportation or on farms a long way from town. Many improvised, removing the engines from their vehicles and hitching the cars to horses instead. Canadians started to call these odd-looking machines "Bennett buggies," after Prime Minister R. B. Bennett, because they thought his economic policies were doing more harm than good.

On February 23, 1909, members of Alexander Graham Bell's Aerial Experiment Association (AEA) dragged the *Silver Dart* onto the ice at Baddeck, Nova Scotia, for what would be the first powered airplane flight in the British Empire. The lightweight wood-and-steel plane took off fairly effortlessly on its second attempt, astonishing those who'd gathered on shore to watch. Although the pilot made flying look easy, he was putting himself at great risk. Just the year before this photo was taken, one member of the AEA had crashed a plane built by the aviation pioneer Orville Wright, becoming the world's first airplane fatality.

The Cold War threat of Soviet bombers over the Far North persuaded the government to fund the production of a sleek fighter jet called the Avro Arrow. Engineers claimed the 1950s jet was the fastest, most sophisticated plane of its time, but cost overruns and possibly even pressure from the United States made the government lose faith and cancel the project. In quashing the Arrow, Canada also killed its own budding aerospace industry, and the country lost hundreds of skilled engineers to the United States. But what most shocked Avro employees was the order to destroy all the finished planes, scale models, and blueprints. "I will always remember the smell of the acetylene torches in the big hangars," said a worker who was there the day the planes were dismantled. "That smell will live with me for the rest of my days."

Canadarm2 hangs off the front of the International Space Station (ISS) like the pincers of some giant mechanical lobster. It's the most critical element in the Canadian Space Agency's Mobile Servicing System, a complex robotic network that also includes the Mobile Base System (a small truck that moves around the outside of the ISS on rails) and the Special Purpose Dexterous Manipulator, or Canada Hand (scheduled to be launched into space in late 2007).

Canadarm2 is a more sophisticated version of the original Canadarm, which flew to space and back aboard shuttle missions and was designed to launch and repair satellites, move cargo, and position astronauts during spacewalks. The new arm has played a critical role in building the ISS — no small feat when you're talking about a structure that's bigger than a football field and is floating around roughly 350 kilometres (220 miles) above the earth. More agile than a human arm, Canadarm2 has been used to extend massive solar panels, attach new modules, and help dock the space shuttle. It can move around the space station by flipping end over end like a Slinky toy or by riding the rails of the Mobile Base System. When the Canada Hand is attached, the arm will be able to hold and manipulate specialized tools, taking over delicate tasks that are currently performed by astronauts during dangerous spacewalks. Eventually, the completed space station will become a launching pad for trips to Mars and beyond.

INTO THE BREACH
Canada at War

Canada has been involved in only a handful of wars in its history, and none — with the exception of the War of 1812, fought long before we were a country — has been waged on Canadian soil. But a look at the wars we have engaged in, and the feelings they have stirred at home, tells us quite a bit about the way this country and its people have changed and evolved.

In 1899, when war broke out between Britain and a group of Dutch settlers in what is now South Africa, there was not much question, at least in English Canada, that we would do our part to help. Most people took it for granted that a colony would support its mother country. When the First World War erupted about a decade and a half later, a similar attitude prevailed. "It is our duty," said Wilfrid Laurier, then the leader of the Opposition, "to let Great Britain know . . . that all Canadians are behind the mother country, conscious and proud that she has engaged in this war, to save civilization from the unbridled lust of conquest and power." But that war was also an opportunity for Canada to show itself on the world stage – and by the time it was over, the country had moved fully out of Britain's shadow.

By 1939, Canada was independent enough to enter the Second World War on its own behalf, by its own decision. But this war stirred more bitter debate at home than the previous one had. After decades of immigration, there were now many Canadians who had no ties at all to Britain, and they saw no sense in travelling halfway around the world just to wage somebody else's war. Others thought that Nazi Germany posed a threat to us all, and that no one anywhere was safe. The debate that followed touched on issues of nationalism, obligations to other nations, language and heritage, and the role Canada – still a young nation – wanted to play in the world.

These same issues would reappear with the conflicts that lay ahead in Korea and Vietnam. But those campaigns were fought far away, in countries that most people here knew nothing about. Many Canadians had lost any taste for war they might once have had, and they longed instead for a world that sought peace through compromise and negotiation, not violence and bloodshed.

These Boer War soldiers, including some members of the Royal
Canadian Regiment, are awaiting treatment at a South African
field hospital during the Battle of Paardeberg in 1900. Paardeberg
was Canada's first victory on a foreign field of conflict. "Fighting
is the easiest part of the campaign," wrote one soldier to his local
newspaper, in a letter that described torrential rains, worn-out uniforms,
and dwindling rations of half-raw meat. But when the time came
to do battle, the men were ready. "Our company suffered far the
most. . . . [But] now it seems this crowd will surrender," he reported.
"The Canadians did it all."

First World War gunners in France fire from behind the Canadian lines on April 9, 1917, the first day of the Battle of Vimy Ridge. The ridge, held by the Germans, was of tremendous strategic importance. The Canadians knew that if they could take it, they would control a great stretch of open country below. Their assault began with a massive artillery barrage that shook the ground like an earthquake and set the night sky alight. That laid the groundwork for an advance that drove the Germans right off the ridge.

Vimy Ridge was the first time our soldiers fought under Canadian (instead of British) command. It was a costly battle — more than 3,500 lives were lost — but the Canadians gained more ground and took more prisoners than the British had been able to do in any previous offensive of the First World War. "The Canadians . . . showed they could fight as well as anyone," wrote one soldier in a proud letter home, "and a little better than [the Germans]." Despite the losses, Vimy Ridge was a great morale-builder. It gave Canadians a tremendous sense of pride in their troops — and a mistaken belief that the war might soon be over.

One of the most famous photographs of Vimy Ridge shows a line
of Canadian soldiers trooping across the endless mud of no man's
land. Intent on their task, they don't even glance at their dead comrades
as they pass or seem to notice the explosions that fill the sky behind them.

Ivor Castle was the official photographer for the Canadian War
Records Office from August 1916 to June 1917. His photographs were
praised for their realistic portrayal of modern warfare, and Castle wasn't
shy about describing the dangers he faced in getting them. "For more
than two miles I had to go through shell-fire, and the ground seemed as
though it had been visited by an earthquake," he once wrote. "The taking
of photographs under such circumstances is a disagreeable business."

We now know that many of Castle's photos were not as authentic
as he claimed. The Vimy Ridge shot, for one, was taken during a training
exercise, not at the battle itself, and the fallen soldiers and plumes of
smoke were added from photographs he took at another time. (If we
could look at the negative with a magnifying glass, we'd even see that
one soldier is thumbing his nose at the camera!) Nevertheless, Castle's
work helped maintain the public's support for the war in its darkest
days, when Canadian casualties were at their highest and a German
victory seemed certain.

Despite the tempting offer of a free trip to Europe, recruitment efforts like this one were not producing enough volunteers to replace Canada's dead and wounded soldiers, so the government introduced conscription – compulsory military service, or the draft. The issue divided the nation. Quebecers, in particular, didn't want to be forced into a conflict that they felt had nothing to do with them. Irate, they rioted in the streets of Montreal, but Prime Minister Robert Borden stood firm. "I would feel that their blood," he wrote of Canada's recent war dead, "and the blood of all the other victims of the war would be on my hands if this [conscription] bill did not pass."

Many people felt that young, healthy men who didn't enlist voluntarily — or, worse yet, who opposed the draft — were shirking their duty to their country. In some communities, women would approach fit-looking young men who weren't in uniform and pin them with a piece of white cloth — a symbol of cowardice. The injured soldiers shown here, two of them leaning on their canes, have done their war service and come home. Their warning to "slackers" is to "beware of the green-eye monster" — in this case conscription, not jealousy.

These military nurses at a Canadian field hospital in France have taken a quick break to cast their ballots in the election of 1917. In August, Parliament had passed legislation giving voting rights (called suffrage) to women in the armed forces, as well as the wives, mothers, and sisters of serving soldiers. Just four months later, these nurses became the first Canadian women to vote in a federal election. Other Canadian women got the right to vote federally on May 24, 1918. But some still had to wait a long time to be able to vote in provincial elections. Women in Quebec didn't win suffrage there until April 1940.

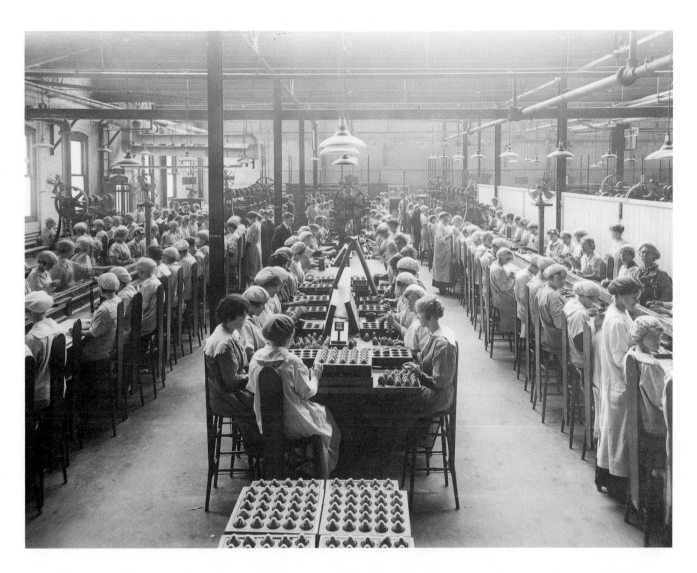

With so many men away on the front lines, women came forward to take their places at home. These women are working in one of the munitions factories that sprang up to make the bullets and shells so desperately needed overseas. These were not easy jobs. Some munitions factories operated around the clock, and they were hot, noisy, dangerous places to work. But the women were proud to be earning their own way, and doing their part for the war effort.

These people are celebrating the Armistice — the peace agreement that ended the war — in the streets of downtown Victoria, British Columbia. The road to peace began with a campaign called the Hundred Days, a series of battles that took place between August 8, 1918, and November 11. Beginning with the Battle of Amiens, in France, a joint Canadian and Australian assault involving aircraft, tanks, and foot soldiers pummelled the German lines. The troops attacked again and again, often in the face of fierce resistance and with staggering casualties. But they persevered, pushing the Germans out of towns and villages all over northern France, and eventually right back across the Belgian border.

People knew that the Hundred Days was the last great push of the war. They expected peace at any time — so much so that these revellers have jumped the gun a little and are celebrating a few days too early. In the midst of war, accurate information was hard to come by, and a rumour out of New York sent them spilling out into the streets on November 7. (In the background, an ad for Victory Bonds urges the boisterous crowd to "Keep the Hun on the run.")

When the Armistice did finally come — on the eleventh hour of the eleventh day of the eleventh month — there was jubilation in all the Allied nations. But every celebration was tinged with sadness. The war had claimed so many young lives — more than sixty thousand from Canada, and almost ten million worldwide — that it was hard not to feel mournful. "It seemed to me that behind the ringing of those peals of joy," said one veteran, "there was the tolling of spectral bells for those who would return no more."

Canadians had only twenty-one years of peace before Hitler's armies invaded Poland and another world war erupted. It was just enough time for the sons of those who survived the First World War to grow to military age. In 1939, factories began gearing up to support yet another war effort – manufacturing fighter planes, weapons, ammunition, and other supplies. Even the uniforms our soldiers would wear into battle had to be hastily stitched together, on foot-powered sewing machines, after Canada declared war on Germany on September 10, 1939.

With so many men heading overseas, their wives, daughters, and girlfriends once again flooded the workforce. More than a quarter of a million women were soon making goods in the war industries, as these welders, employees of the Bren machine-gun factory, are doing. And in this war, women were finally able to serve in the military as something other than nurses as well. Thousands took on administrative and support roles in the armed forces, freeing up male soldiers for combat duty. Although they were paid only a fraction of what their male counterparts made, these female recruits proved to be competent, reliable workers, and that helped open doors for women in the post-war world.

Japan was a new enemy in the Second World War, and fear and long-held anti-Asian feelings quickly threw some Canadians into a state of panic. There were people in British Columbia, in particular, who were convinced that Japanese troops would sail across the Pacific and invade, or that Japanese Canadians would contaminate local drinking water or attack with poison gas. These schoolchildren practising their lessons in gas masks show the extreme lengths some people went to to be ready for this attack when it came. Of course, it never did.

Authorities began rounding up Japanese Canadians and sending them to "protective areas" — really, internment camps — far from the British Columbia coastline. They also seized their property, shutting down businesses and confiscating homes, cars, and hundreds and hundreds of fishing boats, as shown here. No Japanese Canadians were ever charged with taking part in any enemy acts, but most were nevertheless unable to recover what had been taken from them during the war. It took more than forty years, until 1988, for them to win an apology and some meagre financial compensation from the Canadian government.

The Allied raid on Dieppe, a resort town on the coast of France that the Germans had taken over, was meant to be a test run for a future invasion of Europe. It turned into probably the greatest disaster in Canadian military history.

The plan for Dieppe was simple: Canadian troops would be shuttled across the English Channel and deposited on the beach to attack German positions and gain valuable intelligence. The town, the Canadians were told, was lightly defended, and the British would prepare the way with an advance bombing run and provide missile support from Royal Navy battleships.

When the Canadians got to the beach, though, they found a well-fortified town full of German soldiers who seemed to be waiting for them. The British had changed their minds about the bombing run, and they'd also decided that their battleships would be too easy prey for the German airforce. The Canadians waded ashore with almost no support, and the results were predictable. "Bullets flew everywhere," remembered one soldier. "Enemy mortar bombs started to crash down. Around me, men were being hit and bodies were piling up, one on top of the other. It was terrifying."

Of roughly five thousand Canadians who landed on the coast that day, almost fifteen hundred were killed or wounded. Close to two thousand were taken prisoner — including the soldiers seen here, being marched through town by their triumphant German captors while some curious townspeople watch from their balconies in the background.

Dieppe at least taught the Allies what not to do when they launched the D-Day invasion – the first step in driving the Germans out of occupied Europe – on June 6, 1944. This time, they bombarded the German positions in advance, and backed up the invading troops with full naval and air support. These Canadian soldiers are in a landing craft on their way to Juno Beach, near the French town of Courseulles-sur-Mer. The plan, apparently, was for them to cycle their way inland from the beach, but most men abandoned their bicycles within hours. They do look remarkably relaxed, in spite of the danger they're about to face. Huge numbers of men were lost again, but D-Day did prove to be the beginning of the liberation of Europe.

Two young German boys wave a white flag and raise their hands
in surrender to Canadian troops passing through their village.
As they pushed into Germany in the spring of 1945, the Allies saw for
the first time the horror of the concentration camps, where millions
of Jews and other targeted peoples had been killed. "[The camps]
showed where the descent into barbarism can lead," wrote the future
Quebec premier René Lévesque, then working as a war correspondent.
"This was not a chance mishap, but . . . a hell fabricated with great
care. We couldn't believe what we saw."

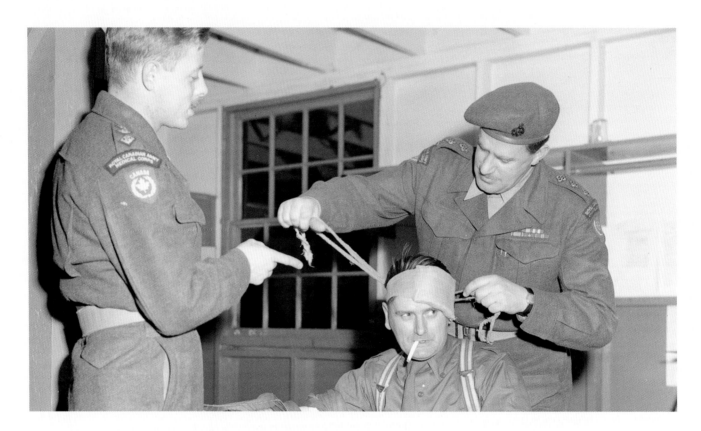

Korea is often called Canada's forgotten war. Technically, it was
never a war at all, but instead was a "police action" designed
to restore peace. Canada was drawn into the conflict – which began
when forces from the Communist north invaded South Korea in
June 1950 – as part of a United Nations mission led by the American
general Douglas MacArthur. Reluctant to commit regular troops to
what it feared might be a prolonged, unpopular struggle (it turned
out to be one of the bloodiest wars in history), the government asked
for volunteers to serve in a Canadian Army Special Force. Many of
those who signed up were veterans from the Second World War, but
some were a bit rusty. Here, a soldier who's about to be sent overseas
realizes that his first-aid technique still needs a little work.

Korea convinced many Canadians of the futility of settling conflicts through war, and of the need for international agencies like the United Nations. When the future prime minister Lester Pearson won a Nobel Peace Prize for his work establishing the first UN Emergency Force – to help resolve a 1956 clash over control of the Suez Canal, in Egypt – Canadians began to think of peacekeeping as their special calling. Since the Suez Crisis, Canadian troops have taken part in many important peacekeeping missions, including those in Cyprus, Rwanda, Haiti, and as shown here, Bosnia. The technology of the military is a lot more sophisticated than it was in the days when those oxen trains carried troops to battle Louis Riel, but the challenges modern Canadian soldiers face are no less complicated.

SOS

Canada in Crisis

Because of its sheer size and its diverse geography – towering peaks in the west, deep and dangerous waters in the east, and frozen wilderness in the north – Canada is at risk of all kinds of natural catastrophes, from floods and rockslides to tornadoes. Other disasters – fires, structural collapses, train derailments – happen through accident or negligence, and could often be avoided. And a few are deliberate acts of vandalism or terrorism.

Disasters make great subjects for photographers because they are so shocking and full of drama. But it's too easy to forget the human stories behind the images. What photos rarely show are the tremendous displays of courage that frequently go hand in hand with disaster – the rescue people at the Springhill Mine who risked their own lives to save the lives of their friends and co-workers, for example, or the railway employee who tapped out a last message to stop a train before Halifax exploded in a ball of flame.

Tragedy often brings people together – even neighbours who hardly know each other will work side by side to save their communities from ruin. Sometimes, the most surprising people turn out to be heroes, dragging victims from burning buildings and rescuing others despite their own terrible injuries. Photographs can bring a distant catastrophe home, inspiring those who haven't been touched by it to reach out to those who have. They can also remind us of the astonishing depths of the human spirit. But no picture can ever resurrect a devastated community or restore a life that's been lost.

On November 18, 1929, an earthquake in the Grand Banks raised a wall of water and sent it racing towards Newfoundland's Burin Peninsula at more than one hundred kilometres (sixty miles) an hour. The tidal wave reached shore with a shuddering crash, according to a St. John's newspaper, "pouring in through door and window and carrying back, in its undertow, home and mother and children." Twenty-nine people were killed, and thousands more were left homeless. As part of the relief effort, this schooner retrieves one house that was washed right out to sea.

377.— CHAMPLAIN ST. DISASTE

Back in 1889, Quebec City's Champlain Street was crushed by the rubble of a rockslide that claimed forty-five lives. It was the fourth time in fifty years that the face of Cap Diamant had given way and come tumbling down on the residents below. The massive pile of rock hurtled down the cliff "with the noise of thunder," reported the local paper, " . . . pushing half a dozen houses out of its way and crushing most of them beneath its weight as though they had been so many paper boxes."

Rockslides were not uncommon elsewhere in Canada either. In 1903, several million tonnes of rock shook loose from Turtle Mountain, in southwestern Alberta, and plunged down the hillside towards the town of Frank. It took just one hundred seconds for the massive slide to bury everything in its path. The Frank slide was the worst in Canadian history, but it was also a story of desperate rescues and great heroics. Seventeen men trapped in the local mine spent thirteen hours digging their way to freedom through almost nine metres (thirty feet) of solid rock. And one rail worker scrambled madly over piles of debris to stop an oncoming train, possibly saving the lives of all aboard.

This dramatic photograph, taken in 1910, shows the *Princess May*, a Canadian Pacific passenger steamer, driven up on some rocks off the coast of Alaska's Sentinel Island. The *Princess May* — with her sister ship, the *Princess Sophia* — regularly carried people and freight from Vancouver to Skagway, Alaska, and back again. But the trip up the Inside Passage could be perilous. The *Princess May* was stranded for almost a month after this grounding, although her cargo and passengers were saved. The *Princess Sophia* wasn't as lucky. In 1918, she ran aground in a storm, almost exactly as the *Princess May* had done. Most people — both on board and on shore — thought the *Sophia* would be stranded for a few days and then towed to safety as soon as the weather improved. Passengers dined as usual, strolled the decks, and gazed at the news photographers who'd come to record the unfolding story. But instead of fading, the storm grew stronger, and the surging waters eventually pushed the ship off the reef, spun her around, and sank her. The *Princess Sophia* was swallowed up so quickly that only a few lifeboats were launched, and those were promptly smashed in the waves or against the rocks. Sadly, all the passengers and crew — more than three hundred people — were lost.

After the tragedy, Canadian Pacific destroyed all its photographs of the *Princess Sophia*. Today, only a handful of grainy images of the doomed ship survive, and none is as spectacular as this photo of the *Princess May* waiting patiently for the storm to pass.

...y... wrecked on Sentinel Island - Alaska . Aug 5th 1910.

Canada's deadliest rail accident occurred on June 29, 1864, when a Grand Trunk train loaded with sleeping passengers went off a swing bridge in St-Hilaire, Quebec. The bridge had been swung open to let a line of barges pass through, but for some reason the engineer ignored the signals telling him to stop. The train, which was filled with newly arrived German and Polish immigrants, plunged through the gap and into the waters of the Richelieu River below. Although the accident claimed ninety-nine victims, it could have been much worse. The train actually landed on one of the barges, which kept many cars out of the water and probably saved countless lives.

Some accidents happen when we are mastering new technology. In 1907, the Quebec Bridge, just outside Quebec City, buckled under its own weight and collapsed. Why? Because engineers had disastrously miscalculated how much weight the structure could support. In memory of the catastrophe, which killed seventy-five workers, Canadian engineering graduates, to this day, are given iron rings to wear. The rings, which some believe are made from the wreckage of the collapsed bridge, are to remind them that they have a responsibility to make sure this tragedy is never repeated.

Fire was a constant threat in early Canada, where buildings were often flimsily constructed, mostly of wood, and placed too close together. Even the Parliament Buildings were not immune. They burned twice — first in 1897, and again in 1916. Many people believed that the second fire, which happened in the middle of the First World War, was the work of German saboteurs. But it was more likely caused by a careless parliamentarian tossing away a smouldering cigar in the paper-strewn reading room. This was the last photo taken before the centre tower collapsed into rubble at about one o'clock on the morning of February 4.

L ike a scene from a movie, a huge black cloud of smoke bears down
   on the main street of the small Ontario mining community of
South Porcupine. The dry spring and hot summer of 1911 had created
ideal conditions for fire in the forests that surrounded the town, and
on July 11, a strong wind whipped up a firestorm. The flames ringed
South Porcupine on three sides, and panicking townspeople fled into
the local lake to escape the choking smoke. Tragically, many of them
actually drowned in their attempt to save themselves from the flames.

Today, firefighting is a high-tech job that relies on aerial ladders and powerful water pumps. In the past, though, small communities often had to count on poorly equipped volunteers and bucket brigades – people passing pails of water from hand to hand – to extinguish a blaze. Not surprisingly, fires were often deadly. The photograph on the right catches the final moments of a Quebec church in 1937. The steeple and cross are still visible above the flames; the rest of the building is all but gone.

In the early morning hours of December 6, 1917, the French munitions carrier *Mont Blanc* — loaded with live ammunition, TNT, and a fuel called benzol — began edging its way into Halifax Harbour. At around the same time, the relief ship *Imo* hoisted anchor and headed for the Atlantic. In the confusion of a busy wartime port, the two ships were soon on a collision course. After a panicked series of horn blasts and shouted warnings, both ships' captains made the fateful error of trying to avoid a crash by turning in the *same* direction. The ships collided, and because of the *Mont Blanc*'s dangerous cargo, they set off what was the world's largest man-made explosion until the Americans dropped an atomic bomb on Hiroshima, Japan, in 1944.

The Halifax Explosion remains the most devastating disaster in Canadian history. The blast climbed high into the sky and was heard as far away as Prince Edward Island. It let loose a fireball that tore through the waterfront streets, wiping out everyone and everything in its path. More than 1,600 people died, and thousands more were injured. In this photograph, of an area of the city that was mercifully spared, shell-shocked citizens wander past some of the hundreds of pine coffins that have been hastily assembled to receive the victims.

These resourceful nuns paddled their way to higher, drier ground
during Manitoba's Red River flood of 1950. They were just two
of about a hundred thousand people who fled Winnipeg when the
river burst its banks and turned the city – and hundreds of kilometres
of surrounding farmland – into a cold and murky inland sea. The
worst night, May 5, was called "Black Friday." Eight dikes were
destroyed that night and four of the city's eleven bridges collapsed
as water overran the downtown.

After Winnipeg's 1950 flood, the province built floodways – channels for diverting overflow water like spring runoff – and adopted other flood-control measures. These protected Winnipeg, but rural areas remained vulnerable. In 1997, when the mighty Red River once again overflowed its banks, it submerged about eight hundred farms – and at least one doghouse – between Winnipeg and the United States border. Sandbag dams became such a common sight that Manitobans – who never lost their sense of humour – took to calling the bags Red River perogies, a nod to the Ukrainian heritage of so many of the province's residents.

Mining coal deep underground, using volatile explosives, is a risky way to make a living. The mine at Springhill, Nova Scotia – the deepest in North America – was the site of three separate disasters, in 1891, 1956, and 1958. These haggard-looking men are two of a hundred lucky survivors of the 1958 explosion, which was set off by a massive "bump," a mining term for a kind of underground earthquake. Most of the survivors were brought out by rescuers the morning after the blast, but almost two dozen were trapped for six or more days. One man was caught in a crawlspace eerily about the size of a coffin. He had no food for the nine days it took to rescue him, and when he was found, his face was black with coal dust, his limbs had seized up from lack of blood circulation, and he'd scratched his fingertips raw trying to claw his way to freedom. Nearby, several more miners had huddled together in a space that left them barely enough room to sit up. These "miracle miners" stayed alive by sucking on pieces of coal and eating small wooden chips they peeled off the mine's support beams.

Soon after the 1958 disaster, the mine at Springhill, considered one of the most dangerous in the world, was shut for good. But today, the abandoned shafts have a second life, providing geothermal power – energy harnessed from water heated deep within the earth – to many local businesses.

Hamilton Dec 1898.

Living in Canada means contending with Mother Nature whether we like it or not. Here, an 1898 ice storm has turned the streets of Hamilton, Ontario, into a winter wonderland. It may look beautiful, but ice can be immensely dangerous and destructive – as residents in New Brunswick, Quebec, and eastern Ontario were to learn exactly a hundred years later.

The ice storm of 1998 shut down bridges and tunnels and toppled millions of trees, almost destroying Quebec's maple-sugar industry in the process. It also pulled down power lines and crumpled hydro towers as if they were made of paper, plunging about four million Canadians into darkness and frigid cold. But the storm brought out the best in people as well. Those who still had electricity took in others – often total strangers – who weren't so lucky. From unaffected areas of the country came donated electrical generators, hand-cut firewood, and the largest peacetime deployment of soldiers in Canadian history.

FUN AND GAMES

Canada at Play

Someone once jokingly described Canada as a place with nine months of winter and three months of poor sledding. It sometimes feels that way on those dark, cold January afternoons that seem to drag on forever. Nowadays, most of us take refuge in our central heating at the sight of the first snowflake and then count the minutes until spring comes. But it wasn't always this way.

The Canadian winter was once a time of rest and recreation. Rivers would freeze, shutting down mills and bringing trade and transportation to a halt. Fields that needed constant attention in the other three seasons lay dormant, giving farmers some hard-earned time off. For most of the population, in fact, winter was a welcome break, a chance to forget about work and start thinking about having fun.

Early Canadians looked to their Native countrymen for

ideas on how to embrace the ice and snow, and Native pastimes like tobogganing and snowshoeing quickly caught on. People would tramp across fields, skate gracefully over ponds, or go hurtling down hillsides on sleds or skis with almost child-like abandon. "A constitution nursed upon the oxygen of our bright winter atmosphere," wrote Lord Dufferin, the governor general in the 1870s, "makes its owner feel as though he could toss about the pine trees in his glee." He was such a committed convert to the season that he even had an ice rink and a toboggan run installed at Rideau Hall, his official Ottawa residence.

Of course, having fun in Canada is a year-round proposition, and we're fortunate to have so many rivers to swim, lakes to sail, and mountains to climb. We've borrowed from our Native neighbours for many of our leisure activities, including our national game, lacrosse, but we've also welcomed sports from around the globe — golf and curling from Scotland, soccer and cricket from England, and from Ireland a game called bandy that morphed into the favourite Canadian game of all, hockey.

Even today, when most of us live in cities, insulated from Mother Nature and the worst extremes of Canadian weather, we continue to define ourselves by the great wilderness that surrounds us. And although we moan and complain and claim to hate it, winter is perhaps still the season we love most of all.

For most of our history, photographers have worked hard to counter the idea of Canada as a wild place stuck in a semi-permanent winter. But the truth is that there's nothing like snow and ice to highlight the majesty of the Canadian landscape. Here, the spray from Quebec's Montmorency Falls has created a giant ice cone for these daring tobogganers to enjoy. Those who were too faint-hearted — or sensible — to try this themselves could hire local children to show them exactly how fast skis or a sled could go.

Many early photographers used composites to capture large groups of people and create a sense of movement in their pictures. To make a composite, a photographer would take portraits of dozens or sometimes hundreds of individuals, cut them out, and paste them to a background. As he posed each person, the photographer had to keep in mind the position of every other person in the image, and those in the background had to be captured on a smaller negative than those in the foreground, to create the proper perspective. After the composite was assembled, an artist usually painted in shadows and highlights — and sometimes colour — to make the whole image look more realistic.

This 1870 composite by William Notman, probably Canada's most famous photographer, recreates a costume party at Montreal's Victoria Skating Rink. To make this composite, Notman had 150 of the party guests come to his studio with their costumes. If you look closely, you can see people in Scottish kilts, several fancy lords and ladies, and even some soldiers and sailors. The fellow above dressed himself up in clothes that he thought a typical Native Canadian would wear — right down to the feathered headdress and what appears to be a tomahawk he's stuck through his wampum belt. You can pick him out in the finished piece as well, aiming his bow and arrow at two terrified-looking women in the bottom right corner.

Those long weeks spent crossing the Atlantic to a new life in Canada could try the patience of even the most tolerant soul. People did whatever they could to fill the hours and escape the boredom of shipboard life. Here, passengers on an immigrant ship called the *Argonaut* have organized, of all things, a potato race to try to make the trip pass more quickly. Notice the two or three amateur photographers hunched over their cameras in the background. By 1900, about when this photo was taken, photography was already an extremely popular pastime — at least among those with time and money to spare.

These women and their overdressed instructor (look at her high-heeled shoes!) have taken over the beach for an early morning exercise class, probably sometime in the 1930s. They make an odd enough sight that they've attracted the attention of not only the photographer but also a small group of onlookers off to the side. It may be the bathing suits as much as the high-kicking calisthenics that have stopped them all in their tracks. They look pretty modest to our twenty-first-century eyes, but the instructor's outfit gives us a sense of just how revealing the women's suits were for the time.

CANADIAN TOPSY-TURVY RAILWAY

The Canadian Pacific Railway was the inspiration for this namesake, the Canadian Topsy-Turvy Railway, a thrill ride that looks pretty similar to a modern-day rollercoaster, even though this photo is more than a hundred years old. The railway – like other new technologies, including the airplane and the automobile – filled turn-of-the-century Canadians with a taste for speed and excitement that could rarely be satisfied. It must have taken the anonymous photographer quite a few tries to get this shot of the exact moment when the car – and its terrified passengers – are suspended from the very top of the loop.

Iceboating was about as fast as a person could go in the early 1900s, when cars were just starting to appear on the roads and high-speed trains were still a dream of the future. It was common to see dozens of large wooden iceboats whooshing across frozen city harbours, their thick canvas sails filling in the breeze. Here, one iceboat proves just how fast it really is by easily outdistancing a motorcycle during an organized race in Toronto around 1908.

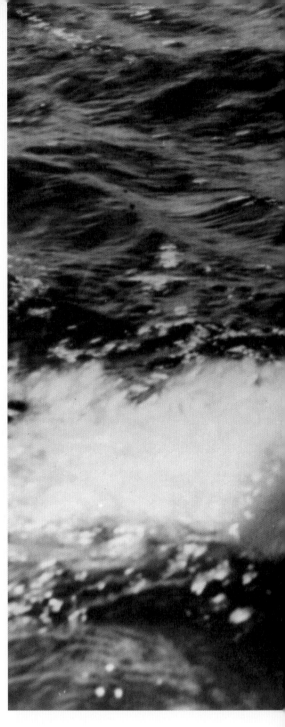

Marathon swimming was a popular sport at Toronto's Canadian National Exhibition (CNE) from the late 1920s right through to the early 1960s. Before they set off, swimmers would slather themselves with grease, which helped insulate the body against the cold temperatures of Lake Ontario and protected the skin from lake creatures like lamprey eels. When sixteen-year-old

Marilyn Bell became the first person to swim across Lake Ontario, in 1954, it was during a CNE-sponsored swim. Pushed about by currents and disoriented by bad weather, she swam almost twice as far as she'd intended, touching a breakwater in Toronto after twenty-one long hours in the water and a mind-boggling seventy thousand strokes.

In its earliest days, hockey was played outdoors, on frozen ponds and rivers. Men and women often played together, without protective padding or helmets (and in the case of these women, in ankle-length skirts!). Team sizes were a fluid thing, determined simply by how many had shown up to play. Some people claim that when it came time to choose teams, the heaviest player was always picked first. If the ice would hold that much weight, the reasoning went, everyone else would be safe too.

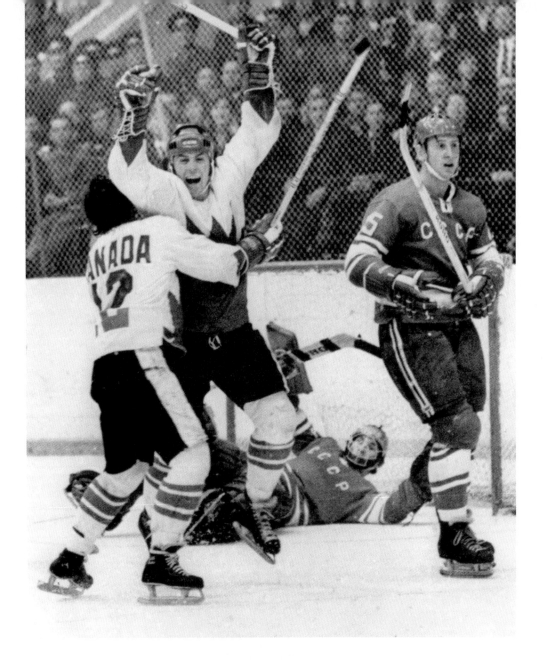

Was it the greatest goal in hockey history? In 1972, Canada took on the Soviet Union in a series of games that everyone thought would be a cakewalk for the professional players from the National Hockey League. Instead, the Soviets gave the Canadians a lesson in puck control that they never forgot. It all came down to the final minute of the final game – and a shot by Paul Henderson that slipped through the goalie's pads and restored every Canadian's faith in our supremacy in the game we gave to the world.

In one of the most heartbreaking moments in Canadian sports history, Ben Johnson (left) was stripped of his 100-metre gold medal at the 1988 Seoul Olympics after testing positive for a banned substance, the steroid stanazolol. It took eight long years for Canada's redemption to come, but, finally, at the Atlanta Olympics in 1996, Donovan Bailey (above) crossed the finish line ahead of all challengers. In just 9.84 seconds, he erased that bleak chapter, saying later that he had run "proudly, cleanly, and with dignity" for his country.

CHARTING THE FUTURE

Canada Comes of Age

P rime Minister Wilfrid Laurier once famously proclaimed that the twentieth century would belong to Canada. "Canada shall be the star," he declared, "to which all men who love progress and freedom shall come." Laurier died in 1919, so he didn't really have the chance to see if his prediction would prove true. But he lived long enough to witness the first great waves of immigration, and the moment when Alberta and Saskatchewan became provinces. He knew that Canadian soldiers had distinguished themselves on the battlefields of France and helped the Allies win the First World War. He watched this underpopulated, mostly rural country take its first tentative steps towards becoming a prosperous, highly developed nation.

Still, the Canada of Laurier's time bears little resemblance to the country we know today. Laurier never knew about the pervasiveness of television or the Internet, or about the horrors of the Second World War and the concentration camps, and the way they changed our perceptions of the world. He missed the Great Depression, Alberta's oil boom, and the collapse of the East Coast fisheries. He never saw the Mounties clash with striking workers in Winnipeg, or experienced the otherworldliness of major cities completely shut down by ice storms and blackouts. He didn't have the chance to celebrate Newfoundland joining Confederation, the creation of Nunavut, or the country turning one hundred years old.

As a committed nationalist, Laurier would have been pleased to know that Canada is now a fully independent nation, with its own flag and its own constitution. But he would have been devastated to learn that his home province, Quebec, had still not signed onto that constitution by the time the century drew to a close. The battle over Quebec's role in Canada – a conflict that consumed so much of "our" century – would have been deeply painful to a man whose motto was "Canada first, Canada last, Canada always."

"Nothing worth having in this life comes easily," wrote another of our great prime ministers, Pierre Trudeau, when he was trying to bring our constitution home. "The creation and development of Canada has been no exception. So many people of differing cultures and languages and local traditions, living on a land which beggars the imagination by its extent and its variety! So many tendencies, all so reasonable, to go our different ways! Yet so much to be gained by . . . understanding and respecting each other's ways, while sharing each other's burdens, in this Canada of ours!"

The search for the Northwest Passage – a mythic sea route through the Arctic to the silks and spices of Asia – had consumed the imagination of explorers and adventurers for centuries. The passage was finally traversed in the early 1900s by Norway's Roald Amundsen, who needed three long years to make the journey, crossing from east to west. Between 1940 and 1942, the *St. Roch*, an RCMP schooner, repeated Amundsen's feat, navigating the passage from west to east and reinforcing Canada's claim to sovereignty in the Arctic at the same time. Here, the *St. Roch* and its crew sit trapped in the icy prison of Boothia Inlet, praying desperately for spring to come. More than once on his historic journey, the ship's captain, Henry Larsen, wondered if he and his men had "come this far only to be crushed like a nut on a shoal and then buried by the ice."

On the morning Newfoundland joined Confederation, April 1, 1949, Prime Minister Louis St. Laurent clambered up some scaffolding at the entrance to the Parliament Buildings and struck the first few chisel strokes to add its coat of arms to those of the other nine provinces. Soon, Newfoundland's two Beothuk warriors had joined Saskatchewan's sheaves of wheat and Manitoba's majestic buffalo on the archway. The process of bringing Newfoundland into Canada had gone quite a bit less smoothly, though. Many islanders would have preferred self-government or closer ties with the United States, and in the provincial capital, St. John's, some greeted the day Newfoundland became a province with black flags and armbands, as if there'd been a death in the family.

A surge in patriotic feeling in the 1960s convinced Prime Minister Lester Pearson that it was time for Canada to have a flag of its own. His announcement pleased almost no one. Many Canadians thought that rejecting the Red Ensign, an unofficial flag that combined the Union Jack and Canada's coat of arms, was equivalent to turning their backs on their British roots, and few liked Pearson's favoured design, which featured three red maple leaves sandwiched between two bands of blue. Some were so furious that they showed up at rallies to express their displeasure with what they mockingly called "Pearson's pennant." In typical Canadian fashion, it fell to a parliamentary committee to sort out the whole mess, and do it quickly. The design they chose — one single maple leaf between two bands of red — wasn't instantly popular, but over the years it has become the most loved symbol of Canada, and the one most recognized around the world.

All that new patriotism reached a fever pitch at Expo 67 in Montreal. The world's fair, which Montreal's mayor, Jean Drapeau, had dreamed up to celebrate Canada's hundredth birthday, in 1967, was a futuristic take on the global village. More than fifty million people came to see it, zipping around the fairgrounds on the monorail or swinging slowly through the sky in cable cars. Visitors could catch a puppet show in the Czech pavilion; make a simulated journey to the centre of the earth on a ride called the Gyrotron; tour Habitat, Moshe Safdie's cube-shaped housing complex; or watch a film in Buckminster Fuller's twenty-first-century dome, which became a symbol of the fair itself. Even the Expo site – on two islands built in the middle of the St. Lawrence River with landfill from Montreal's subway system – seemed ahead of its time. The fair was, declared the *Montreal Star*, "the most staggering Canadian achievement since this vast land was finally linked by a transcontinental railway."

Still, not everyone was happy. Quebec separatists chose to mark Canada's centennial with the slogan *"100 ans d'injustice"* ("One hundred years of injustice"), and when France's president, Charles de Gaulle, came to visit the fair, he ignited a storm of controversy by crying out, *"Vive le Québec libre!"* ("Long live a free Quebec!"). To separatists, de Gaulle's rallying call was like an international stamp of approval on their sovereigntist ambitions. But to most of the rest of Canada, it was outrageous meddling that marred an otherwise triumphant year.

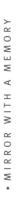

Some separatists went well beyond slogans and placards. In 1963, a group calling itself the Front de libération du Québec (FLQ) had begun a violent campaign for Quebec independence. FLQ members placed bombs in mailboxes around Montreal, stole cash and weapons, and attacked McGill University and the Montreal Stock Exchange. In October 1970, they kidnapped two men – a British trade commissioner named James Cross, and the Quebec labour minister, Pierre Laporte. Laporte was found murdered in the trunk of a car just a week later – a crime that horrified and enraged most Canadians. Claude Ryan, a prominent journalist who later became the leader of the Quebec Liberal Party, called the killing a "cruel assassination" that "struck us like a blade, cutting without pity into what we hold most sacred."

The Quebec government sought help from Ottawa in coping with this "October Crisis," and Prime Minister Pierre Trudeau invoked the War Measures Act. This decades-old law gave the federal government exceptionally broad powers to deal with "war, invasion or insurrection" on Canadian soil. Trudeau used it to send the army in to patrol Montreal, to outlaw the FLQ, and to arrest hundreds of Quebecers and hold them in jail without charging them with any crimes.

The sight of armed troops in the streets of one of our biggest cities shook Canadians to their core, and some felt that, in using the War Measures Act, the government had gone too far. But James Cross was freed after two months of captivity, the FLQ collapsed, and the idea of using terrorism to promote Quebec independence was completely discredited.

Rain and hail greeted the Queen on April 17, 1982, when she came to Ottawa to sign the royal proclamation that made our constitution into law. It was the moment that Canada truly became a sovereign nation, free of its legal ties to Great Britain. As always, however, the moment was not without detractors. Quebec's premier René Lévesque, unhappy that his province had no special status in the constitution, refused to sign on to it or to be present at the ceremony to mark its patriation, and he ordered all Quebec flags flown at half-mast. But Pierre Trudeau, who had laboured for years to bring the constitution home, refused to allow Lévesque to ruin the day. "[This] marks the end of a long winter," he declared, "the breaking-up of the ice-jams, and the beginning of a new spring."

Like Newfoundland fifty years earlier, Nunavut — a new territory carved out of the eastern half of the Northwest Territories — took its place in Confederation on April Fool's Day, in 1999. Stretching from the Manitoba border to the North Pole, Nunavut (which means "our land" in Inuktitut, the Inuit language) would be the world's thirteenth-largest nation if it were an independent country. The territory is rich in natural resources, and mining for gold, zinc, copper, and even diamonds is a major industry. It's an extreme landscape — rough Canadian Shield covered by a very thin layer of soil and interlaced with hundreds of glacial rivers — and temperatures can drop well below -35°C, cold enough to freeze unprotected skin in minutes. In fact, Nunavut has the unhappy distinction of being the site of the lowest windchill levels ever recorded. In the community of Pelly Bay, a strong January gale once made -51°C feel like a mind-boggling -92°C!

When Terry Fox lost his leg to bone cancer, he resolved to find a way to raise money for cancer research. In April 1980, he dipped his artificial leg in the ice-cold Atlantic and set out to cross Canada on foot, running the equivalent of a marathon every single day. Slowly, his determination and courage captured the imagination of Canadians, and the sparse crowds that had watched him pass through the streets of St. John's, Newfoundland, had grown to thousands of screaming fans by the time he reached Ontario. As he ran through communities big and small, members of his tiny support team worked the lines of onlookers, collecting bucketfuls of cash for his cause. When he reached the halfway point of his run, in Thunder Bay, Ontario, he had raised almost $2 million.

But Terry Fox would run no farther. In Thunder Bay, he learned that his cancer had spread to his lungs. At a press conference, he vowed to fight it, saying, "This just intensifies what I did. It gives it more meaning. It'll inspire more people." He was right. Before he died the following year, at just twenty-two, his goal of collecting one dollar for every Canadian had been reached, and he had united this country in a way no one else had ever done.

In the wake of the October Crisis, new champions of Quebec separation emerged. These were writers and painters and politicians, and unlike the FLQ, they did not resort to terrorism. They believed they could achieve independence by peaceful means. When the separatist René Lévesque and his Parti Québécois were elected to govern the province in 1976, separation seemed certain. A referendum on sovereignty-association – which would let Quebec gain political independence while maintaining an economic relationship with Canada – was set for May 1980. It was such a divisive issue that people on the same block, and even within the same family, suddenly found themselves in bitter conflict. After a hard-fought and sometimes nasty campaign, those who said *"Non"* to sovereignty-association won 60 percent of the vote. Quebec would stay in Canada – at least for now.

When a second Quebec referendum rolled around in 1995, the rest of Canada decided to show the province what a valued member of the family it really was. On October 27, as many as a hundred thousand people converged on Montreal to rally in support of Canadian unity. They may have just saved the day, for the referendum results could not have been any closer: this time, the *Non* side won with just 50.6 percent of the vote. "There are not many countries in the world where citizens can debate — peacefully, calmly, and without violence — the very existence of the country itself," said Prime Minister Jean Chrétien at the end of one great nail-biter of a night. "Once again, we have shown the entire world our country's great values of tolerance, openness, and mutual respect." Although it had taken a few hard knocks, Confederation emerged stronger and more relevant than ever.

Photo Credits

Every effort has been made to trace the ownership of copyrighted materials contained in this book. Information that enables the publisher to correct any reference or credit line in future additions will be welcomed.

For reasons of space, the following abbreviations have been used.

AM: Archives of Manitoba, Winnipeg
AO: Archives of Ontario, Toronto
BCA: British Columbia Archives, Vancouver
CPRA: Canadian Pacific Railway Archives
CTA: City of Toronto Archives, Toronto
GA: Glenbow Archives, Calgary
HBCA: Hudson's Bay Company Archives, Winnipeg
LAC: Library and Archives Canada, Ottawa
MM: McCord Museum, Montreal
NA: Notman Archives, McCord Museum, Montreal
TRPA: The Rooms Provincial Archives Division,
      Newfoundland and Labrador
VPL: Vancouver Public Library, Vancouver

HALF TITLE PAGE
CTA, Fonds 1244, Item 3541

TITLE PAGE
LAC PA-138521

CONTENTS
LAC PA-122520

INTRODUCTION
6: CTA, Fonds 1244, Item 659; *9*: NPA MP-0000.489.2, 1850; *10*: LAC PA-028457/Notman Studio (Halifax)

BUILDING A NATION
12: LAC C-003693/Alexander Ross; *15*: LAC C-000733/George P. Roberts; *17*: LAC C-000773/Samuel McLaughlin; *18*: LAC C-078979; *19*: GA NA-249-25; *20*: GA NA-249-76; *21*: GA NA-250-14; *22*: LAC PA-118754/O. B. Buell; *24*: LAC PA-023141/Dept. of Mines and Technical Surveys; *25*: LAC PA-032137/Albertype Company; *26*: LAC C-003693/Alexander Ross; *27*: LAC C-014115; *28*: GA NA-876-3; *29*: LAC C-005142/E. A. Hegg; *31*: LAC PA-020904/John Woodruff; *32*: LAC C-047042/Pringle and Booth; *33*: LAC PA-041785/Isaac Erb

STORM AND STRIFE
34: AM Foote Collection (N2762); *37*: LAC C-083423/James Inglis; *39*: MM MP-1993.6.2.30, *Troops on the March, Northwest Rebellion, Qu'Appelle Valley, SK*, 1885; *40*: GA NA-3205-5; *41*: LAC C-001879/O. B. Buell; *42*: GA NA-964-22; *44*: AM Foote Collection (N2762); *45*: AM Winnipeg Strike 29 (N12317); *46*: GA ND-3-6742; *47*: GA NA-1831-1; *48*: LAC C-029399; *49*: GA NA-3622-20; *50*: AO I0003697; *51*: Canapress/Shaney Komulainen

FROM HERE TO THERE
52: GA NA-1753-4; *55*: CTA, Fonds 1244, ITEM 3501; *56*: LAC PA-138573/Charles Horetzky; *57*: HBCA 1987/363-Y-2/56 (R. A. Talbot, photographer); *59*: BCA A-00348; *60*: CPRA

A.15515; *61:* GA NA-1255-18; *62:* GA NA-428-1; *63:* GA NA-1753-4; *64:* GA NA-33-16; *65:* LAC PA-154122/B. Brooks/National Film Board of Canada; *66:* GA NA-1790-2; *67:* GA NA-2256-1; *68:* LAC PA-122520; *69:* courtesy of Ron Page; *71:* Canadian Space Agency (www.space.gc.ca)

INTO THE BREACH
72: VPL 44965; *75:* LAC C-006097/Reinhold Thiele; *76:* LAC PA-001879/Dept. of National Defence; *79 (top):* LAC PA-001086; *(bottom):* LAC PA-001020; *80:* CTA, Fonds 1244, Item 721; *81:* CTA, Fonds 1244, Item 726; *82:* LAC PA-002279/William Rider-Rider; *83:* LAC PA-024435/Dept. of National Defence; *84:* BCA F-05321; *86:* LAC PA-116362/A. C. Kells; *87:* LAC E000760329/National Film Board of Canada; *88:* VPL 44965; *89:* LAC PA-037467/Dept. of National Defence; *91:* LAC PA-200058; *92:* LAC PA-133757/Gilbert Alexander Milne; *93:* LAC PA-113697/Alexander M. Stirton; *94:* LAC PA-179972/Dept. of National Defence; *95:* Canapress/Tom Hanson

SOS
96: LAC PA-029808/Henry Peters; *99:* TRPA A2-149, *Tidal wave disaster, Nfld,* Nov. 1929/S.H. Parsons & Sons [postcard #351]; *100:* LAC PA-023895/J. E. Livernois; *101:* LAC PA-052095/Dept. of National Defence; *103:* LAC C-000673; *104:* LAC C-003285/Antoine Bazinet; *105:* LAC C-009766; *106:* LAC C-010079/J. B. Reid; *107:* LAC PA-029808/Henry Peters; *108:* LAC PA-130009/John Boyd; *109:* LAC PA-027465; *110:* NSARM N-4273; *112:* AM Floods 1950 16 (N16103); *113:* Canapress/Chris Procaylo; *115:* LAC PA-

177106/Fednews telephoto; *116:* LAC C-035838/Edwin A. Gaviller; *117:* Canapress/Jacques Boissinot

FUN AND GAMES
118: LAC PA-105057/John Boyd; *121:* LAC PA-138521/ Alexander Henderson; *122:* MM N-0000.68.1, *Skating Carnival, Victoria Rink, Montreal, QC,* painted composite, 1870; *123:* MM I-43612.1, *Mr. Reynolds as "Quewaygoosquequamteros,"* posed for a composite, Montreal, QC, 1870; *124:* MM MP-0000.25.20, *Potato Race on the "Argonaut,"* about 1900; *125:* LAC PA-105057/John Boyd; *126:* MM MP-0000.25.1032, *Canadian Topsy-Turvy Railway,* about 1900; *127:* CTA, Fonds 1244, Item 450; *128:* CTA, FONDS 1244, Item 1028B; *129:* Canapress; *130:* LAC C-079313/H. J. Woodside; *131:* Canapress; *132:* LAC PA-175370/Ted Grant; *133:* Canapress/COC/Claus Andersen

CHARTING THE FUTURE
134: Canapress/Journal de Quebec; *137:* GA NA-2821-7; *138:* LAC C-006255/National Film Board; *139:* LAC PA-136147/Duncan Cameron; *141:* LAC E000995990; *142:* PA-11747; *144:* LAC PA-140706/Robert Cooper; *145:* Canapress/Kevin Frayer; *147:* Canapress/Boris Spremo; *148:* Canapress/Journal de Quebec; *149:* Canapress/Ryan Remiorz

INDEX
155: LAC C-033462/Borden-Clarke; *156:* NA View-3094, *Castle Crags and Hazel Peak,* Banff, AB, 1897.

Arctic Ocean

Northwest Passage

MELVILLE ISLAND

VICTORIA ISLAND

Yukon River

Boothia Inlet

NUNAVUT

YUKON

○ Dawson

Klondike River

Pell

Whitehorse ○

*Chilkoot
Pass*

NORTHWEST
TERRITORIES

C A N A D

Inside Passage

BRITISH
COLUMBIA

ALBERTA

MANITOBA

Pacific Ocean

Fraser River

*Cariboo
Mountains*

Rocky Mountains

Edmonton ○

SASKATCHEWAN

*Rogers
Pass*

○ Duck Lake

Batoche ○

Port Moody ○
Vancouver ○
○ Victoria

○ Craigellachie

○ Spuzzum

○ Calgary

○ Saskatoon

*Turtle
Mountain*

Fort Macleod ○

○ Swift Current

○ Regina

Dufferin ○
Winnipeg ○
Holland ○

Red River

*Lake of
the Woods*

○ Frank

U S A

GREENLAND

BAFFIN ISLAND

Northwest Passage

Hudson Bay

A

LABRADOR

St. John's
NEWFOUNDLAND
Burin
Peninsula

QUEBEC

PRINCE
EDWARD
ISLAND   Baddeck
                 Charlottetown
NEW
BRUNSWICK   Springhill

ONTARIO   Saint
                 John   Halifax

                 NOVA SCOTIA

                 Quebec City
South   St-Hilaire
Porcupine
Thunder   Montreal
Bay   Oka   Richelieu River
         Ottawa River
                         Ottawa   Atlantic Ocean
                 Kingston
Barrie
Toronto   Lake Ontario
Hamilton

INDEX

A Note on the Type

The text in this book is set in Centaur. This Old Style typeface was designed by Bruce Rogers in 1915 for the book *Le Centaure*, by Maurice De Guerin, published by the Metropolitan Museum of New York. He later adapted the type for machine typesetting. In 1935, the *Oxford Lectern Bible* was set in Centaur. Rogers often designed typefaces exclusively for specific books.